Active Gods

Active Gods

Poems

MICHAEL J. HENRY

AN IMPRINT OF BOWER HOUSE

DENVER

Author Photo by Don Peifer

Library of Congress Cataloging-in-Publication Data
is available upon request.

ISBN: 978-1-938633-44-7

10 9 8 7 6 5 4 3 2

for Em and Jo
and
Andrea

. . . and he too had proceeded for some time upon the mere power
of his own mind. Then he began to look, himself, toward
the collective phenomena. As his own self, he had opened
his mouth and uttered some delightful verses.
But then his heart failed him. Ah, Humboldt, how sorry I am.
Humboldt, Humboldt—and this is what becomes of us.

—Saul Bellow, *Humboldt's Gift*

TABLE OF CONTENTS

I

PRAYERS 1

AT THE OPTOMETRIST 2

I WAS MOPPING THE FLOOR AS THE
SMITHS PLAYED ON MY IPOD 3

LIKE EMILY DICKINSON 5

A DAY IN THE LIFE OF BOYS 6

BIRTH ORDER 7

THE STORY OF L 10

SERIOUS TALK 11

CHAINS 13

ACTIVE GODS 15

II

AUGUST, PUBLIC POOL 21

SEPTEMBER SONG 22

CRACKED POLYSTYRENE MAN 24

ANOTHER PRAYER 25

EXPECTATIONS 26

FIVE OBSTRUCTIONS 27

GO TO SLEEP 29

DEAR JOSHUA 30

BULLIES   32

DIM LANDS OF PEACE   34

SEAM   36

ARTHROPODA, INSECTA, LEPIDOPTERA   38

MONSTER POEM   39

III

BLIZZARD AND CROW   45

UPON READING ALL OF CHRIS OFFUTT'S BOOKS   46

USEFUL   47

TO SYLVIA PLATH   48

THE RETURNING PATRIARCH   49

SOLO RENGA   51

MEMOIR OF THE IMAGINED LOVED ONES   53

BUTCHER IN THE NURSING HOME   62

TORNADO   63

INCESSANTLY   64

AFTERGLOW   65

POEM BEGINNING WITH LINES FROM BOB DYLAN   66

I

PRAYERS

Each prayer you whisper is a small bird
rising up, alighting on a branch in the tree
of desire, twisted gray arms, flashing leaves.

These birds will not enter heaven,
will not lose themselves in bright clouds, or run
into picture windows. They hover

and settle in the ivy wall along
the garden, their small voices ringing bells,
their flitting nerves unseen.

You know their closeness each day,
wingbrush against your cheek when raking
the leaves, a shock of breath. At dawn

they wake you, their conversations
a chatter of words without punctuation
or denouement. When you gave them up—

on your knees, in flannel pajamas,
your hands pressed together, smooth
candle-flame of fingers—you believed

they would come to rest in God's ear
and make your life something else
than what it is. But you know, *you know*:

they are just gray-brown finches, with hearts
like ours, searching for seed, building
downy nests in the eaves of the house.

AT THE OPTOMETRIST

That night alive with signs and stars,
I opened myself to the gentle indifference of the world.
—Albert Camus, *The Stranger*

The eye doctor led me to the chart
and I always thought the top letter
was E so I said E and she said *Wrong,*
try again. So I actually looked
and got it right (it was H),
went down a few rows and then—
isn't this always the story—
it all got muddled and I could not say
which was which or what
was what so I tried my best,
squinting, hopeful.
The doctor said I wasn't
20/20 anymore, of course not.
I'm not a kid, my cells are growing
old, ragged, unsupple,
littered with mutations and false
codons. Anyway, after a while I got
my eyeglass prescription and fell
into the murderous summer noon,
dazzled by all the color, my pupils
big black holes sucking in the world.
I stood woozy on the bland
sidewalk as everything flowed past
into the past, shimmering
and blurred and—story
of my life—there was nowhere
I could think to turn,
no DNA sequence prescribing
what I was supposed to do next.

I WAS MOPPING THE FLOOR AS THE
SMITHS PLAYED ON MY IPOD

and then I tipped the stupid bucket
over and the water unraveled
a quick gloss across the floor.
Spillage. Pilloried. Blasted mess,
bastard aqua, non sequitur.

Yes, I do go about things
the wrong way.
Why do my nice dreams and snappy
ideas always flutter away?
One dream I've kept: a cave
in the woods, deep, faraway.
In there with me, a bear sleeps,
the snow deepens.
The bear I am: mind of no
mind, slow heart, stink fur.

You know, I'd like to watch
Jeremiah Johnson again,
someday soon, maybe
also *Dances with Wolves*,
a double-wonder frontier feature.
The endless prairie carpet,
all gorgeous grasses and

undulations. I love the wagon
driver, the guy from *Murphy Brown*,
gnawing hard-boiled eggs. His exquisite
corpse, shocked through with arrows,
one a flagpole for his vitals.
South Dakota, Kansas, not true

mountains but an approximation
of them. I'm done mopping now and
this is not a clean floor but it's
almost there, slippery as ice.
Long oceanic horizon, vast sky,
drying linoleum. How soon is now?

I dunno. Those movie skies care
less than less about us, the real sky is
a vast dome inside
the Great Turtle's shell, the place
I wish to be for all time. Because
I am human and I need to be loved,
just like everybody else does.

LIKE EMILY DICKINSON

From a distance
I am cool and remote,
a silhouette in the window
of the old house.

To be honest, I feel
slow and sick,
my heart aches
in small increments.

But enough of me
and my ailments—
what are you

looking for?
The kiwis,
the navel oranges
you bought yesterday?

(They are in the bowl
on the dining room table.)

These days, ice is
forming on the lake
and soon I will walk out,
onto the white,
my eyes burning.

Cool and remote
you are, as well.
Therefore, I will
not ask you
to come with me.

A DAY IN THE LIFE OF BOYS

At all hours we ran wild
through the neighborhood.
Goal was a hockey net, or a bucket
to kick, or Corny Paul's oak tree.
The games proceeded and evolved.

They lasted days, sometimes.
When we lost, we scraped knees,
we bloodied noses. We ran
home crying and rageful.
When we won, we strutted down
the apex of the street,
psyched at our badassness.

One day we biked to the dead end
field. We hunted grasshoppers,
coddled them in our palms, let them
launch back into the tendrils.
Then Lucky Ray snagged a praying mantis,
took her home in a jar, dropped her
green akimbo body into an empty aquarium,
built a twig-and-grass jungle-gym
for her to play on. For an hour

we stared at her bland orb eyes.
Then Ray tossed in a grasshopper,
and we learned. How smooth and quick
she caught and ate, how quick
and smooth the earth turns
because there is always hunger,
always a winner and a loser.

BIRTH ORDER

First
You were the mistake, the one who crashed
the wedding without an invite, in utero.

You trudged to school all by your lonesome.
You got the brunt of everyone's
confusion, their figuring out how to work
all the levers and buttons.

Later, you popped your window-screen and snuck
into the night to do bad things.
You crashed Mom's Galaxie wagon in the ditch.
Busted bones, circling stars, Venus and Mars.

They named you The Wild One, The Floozy.
You wished you were bland and tasteless
like everybody else, like all the nobodies.

Second

Middle child, they were too spent to give a bother,
so says your tweedy mumbling psychotherapist.

You wanted the award for Most Prettiest,
wanted to have a superior thinking machine,
piston the blood, whirl the brain,
vault across the synapse.

You were not impulse made,
you were not the one they shouted at,
though you sometimes wish they would have
boomed and smacked your cheek.
To suffer something, at least.

When you won the spelling bee,
was anyone there in the dark auditorium?
No matter. You couldn't see anyway.

But the winning word
still thrums your heart: *delicacy.*

Third

So, so, so. They don't like the histrionics,
so cut it out, for cripessakes.

Any toy you wanted, you got.
Whatever hour you snuck back
into the house, no problem.
You are their last best wish,
the thing they'll get right,
finally, Jesus Christ—*Don't say*
G_d's name in vain, it's not polite.

Their hope is a heavy ingot full
of anvils trussed onto your back
and you are running up the endless
hill. You think you're the only one
in the race, but the pack is stomping
behind you, and they are growing close,
closer. The whole family's there,

to watch. They clap and holler—
Run, darling boy, run,
run G_d dammit run.

THE STORY OF L

L stumbled into the crypt and was frightened by the truth
of the dark air, though once her eyes adjusted she thought
to stay awhile. She shut the heavy door,

sat on a cold marble bench, gazed at dusty corners,
the finely made stained-glass, the light in
geometries, flowers of gold. L shuddered,

wondered when flesh-eating worms would come
oozing through. Outside, her kids wandered the green
meadows as the dolorous trees lay down their shadows.

Those kids loved her after all, could not imagine a day
without her, did not know how they'd survive the morning rush,
the fall of night, the mountains of laundry and cliffs of dish.

They called out her name, stepping across the many
grassy graves. They touched the rough stones and hieroglyphs,
gazed through the thick frosted windows of each crypt.

L lay down on stone and crossed her hands over her heart.

SERIOUS TALK

—for Matt

You and I settle in against the dark
wood bar as The Replacements'
"Here Comes a Regular" pulls us into the ease
we used to know. In our late 20s,
we are sage men who talk of big things:
summer plans, grad school, women
and their complaints, and then,
eventually, solemnly, because we are
serious dudes, our parents. How when
they're gone, *they're gone*. The absurdity
of it. Where the hell did they go?
And how lonely or inscrutable
they were when they were here,
when they still wore shoes,
not those final casket shoes,
the ones with scratched and burdened soles,
which, come on now, is a word we are
too wise to consider a worthy symbolic
homophone, so hokey and overdone.
And we confess to each other: how lonely are we?
Pretty damn lonely. Mostly when the season
is brutally cold or killer hot, when our lives
are chugging onward but no one
comes knocking or pens us a letter.
We sip the Bass Ale from the bottle,
taking our medicine, doctor's orders.
We are through with purge and drama,
with idiot intoxicated weeping and wall
punching, we are done with driving fast
and drunk down blurry streets.

Like Bishop says, the art of losing isn't hard
to master, and we've had lots of practice.
An hour glides by, then another.
The buzz washes over us with a sweet,
rocking undertow and the place
is suddenly packed and loud.
We run our hands along the smooth shores
of the fine wood and order another round.
Matty, you and I are brothers from
Buffalo, NY, and like all men of this city
we drink to make it feel less like disaster,
drawing up vague but earnest plans
to forge and hammer a silvery booster rocket,
to someday blast us into a most flawless orbit.

CHAINS

I yank the chain of the dog I am
walking and she heels, then strains
toward a smell that blooms
at the base of the street lamp which is
not yet lit, though it's getting dark.
As a kid, such illumination
was my call to go home, triggered
by dusk, my play done for the night.
In the dog's neck there are
batteries and a wire
augured into her heart: a pacemaker.
She used to faint then flail
on her back like a panicked
turtle. Now she is still freaky but
not as. The pacemaker that keeps
her beat in line was pulled from a dead guy,
recycled to save my dog's life.
Someone took it out of the cadaver,
cold, blood spattered, weirdly discolored.
I imagine someone washed it
in antiseptic, someone packed it
and shipped it to the vet who snaked
the thin wires into my dog's heart ever so deftly.
Someone originally maybe sawed
the guy's chest open, his family
waiting in a room somewhere nearby,
probably watching The Price is Right
or some such, his blood flowing through tubes
into a mechanical pump then back
into his body via more tubes.

Some doctor did that, maybe listening
to some music. Classical, or easy country,
or new age, or The Beatles even.
Before that, someone in Germany
or South Korea or Minnesota made
the thing, threaded the fragile mother
board with needle-nosed pliers,
fitted the semiconductor,
soldered the titanium case,
anode, cathode, capacitor.
People made all this, they put it in,
they took it out, they fiddled
with it to make it work,
like God in his six-day mania.
All so I can walk my dog, who was
probably made by pure dog lust
since she's a mixed breed, and like her
aren't we all made from desire,
all want and need and sex and hope,
us and everything we touch?

ACTIVE GODS

Sitting on a park bench by the Peace Bridge,
along the Niagara River, in Buffalo, New York

Stone and iron moor the bridge and while
cars and trucks chug over, water roils under,
14 miles an hour, white-capped and fierce.

When driving over, Mother's command
to us kids was to plug our noses,
as if Dad might lose it, was sure to

careen the Galaxie wagon over the curb,
tearing through the rail, to plunge.
He was our one true god, the one

who brought us in, and, he sometimes
said, the one who could take us out.
Now, as I watch cars glide over

and reconsider the risks,
a future slowly reveals itself:
moving into an old brick house

where surely there will be a wife
and surely there will be some children
tearing the place apart, little girls

who sing of bridges in London,
cherubs who'll weep in cars, the sun
too bright in their eyes, who'll make bridges

out of Legos, who'll wiggle and squirm
generally, and someday I'll contemplate
the fluid cascade of their golden

or maybe red hair, their quick legs
pistoning across a beach somewhere,
a sandy tilted shelf I've brought them to,

me being their active god.
Only then will I understand current
and spindrift as the lake revels

around their ankles at the shore's edge,
gentle waves frothing and repetitive.
And maybe that's all this is:

a crossing over, a giving in,
hoping to find devotion and
belonging on the other shore.

II

AUGUST, PUBLIC POOL

Children swarm under the tower. A hammer
ticks on steel high above, where a massive bucket tilts.
Farther, farther. Almost there. By the false blue
shoreline, three teenage girls bronze their backs.
Boys walk past, flexed and puffed, swallow hard,
lick dry lips. Everything is tease and
anticipation. My little girls are in the mass, waiting.
A bell finally gongs, the bucket tips and spills
chlorinated molten silver on the masses. There are
screams and shouts, and then, it's done, for now.
A lanky boy cannonballs into the deep end.
A mother floats on a tube, eyes closed,
twin pony-tailed daughters ferrying her along the lazy
river. If I were more—more *something*—I might
grab my wallet, go buy a Popsicle or
Cherry Coke. Sweetness burning my throat, ease all
around, the sun going down gold and intimate.
But I've had my life of wanting and sometimes getting,
and even though part of me wants to never leave,
the pretty-boy lifeguards have already begun
to stack chairs. Closing time. My girls scurry up,
blue-lipped and shivering. They want
chocolate cones at Dairy Queen and I won't say no.

SEPTEMBER SONG

—for Garrett Ammon

The guy's name is Collin; it's scripted
on his black shirt in bold red thread.
Collin says my tire's all chewed up, it's done for.
Outside the chain coffee shop, I wait
in the floppy chaise, the constant hum
of the highway looms and the sky is blue
and crystalline—typical for September
at this fine, thin altitude. I sip my
gigantic mocha and feel my teeth
softening. I know it's getting late
and I sense I might have missed something,
time is rolling downhill in the dark,
on rails. Dear September, before-winter
lodger, monk of summer remnants, still
mostly alive, don't be done for.
There's the song where the singer asks
to be woken when you end, as if
this cusp of decay is too heavy to bear,
as if clarity of sky and hushing highway
and tired crickets and balding tires
blowing out at high speed are too much
to abide, and thoughtlessness, or sleep,
or coma—choose your favorite state—
is to be preferred. But I'm here and awake
as Collin with his pretty spiked hair
is replacing my desiccated tire
and giving me a balance, a new black foot
under warranty, cranking it tight
onto the faded Subaru, the jalopy
with the abraded driver seat,

barking struts, and buzzing speakers.
September, my friend, I pray it will never
be too late for us. I pray we'll never need
denial nor slumber, us with our mutual
affection for the bitter and the sweet,
for the sentimental demise
of all things, this frayed and faded
jacket we covet and wear so easy.

CRACKED POLYSTYRENE MAN

Wishes he could stop falling apart
in the dry air. His hands

pull back the brocade curtains,
and on the street, everyone

presses on, weighted like stone in
overcoats and umbrellas, streets aglow.

Six o'clock. A car on the street
shudders to a start, puff of smoke.

Tonight, all around, overwhelming questions
will be whispered across pillows.

He is nowhere, behind a locked door.
Rain ticks against the window

and he grows ever more white,
bleached molecules of phenyl

and carbon, hydrogen and
and van der Waals attraction.

His shape will not decay
though he wishes to be buried

and never dug up. Just one more
lonely man, weight zero, a man

crudely made, indestructible yet brittle,
built to last forever and then some.

ANOTHER PRAYER

You don't need to figure it out.
Give in to the low sun and the
bickering kids in the other
room. Let sundown come, let it be
a sad, bland one, why the hell not?
Let grief—over nothing, over
everything—sweep the air in
a thousand brilliant hues, let it
pulse the heart, the hands.
You are not in control, sometimes,
so what? You miss so much of what
is gone, but desire is sticky and
not always sweet. Let everyone
else write their long, tragic memoirs,
let them review the bullet points
and meditations, the cloying
drag of life, how they bolt-cut the
chain of their own special anchor,
untethering. Let them weep for
their loss. You've got your own past
to enjoy, grieve, bury, love, forget.

EXPECTATIONS

A Found Poem

Though we had expected
to be able to send
this item to you,
we've since found
that it is not
available from any
of our sources

at this time. We realize
this is disappointing news
to hear, and we
apologize
for the inconvenience
we have
caused you.

We must also
apologize for the length
of time it has taken
us to reach
this conclusion.
Until recently,
we had still hoped
to obtain
this item
for you.

We have cancelled
this item
from your order.

FIVE OBSTRUCTIONS

I. Color
The morning light
kills at low angles
and I am creaky
but hopeful,
aspirational even.
My eyes can't focus
and I kind of like it
that way.

II. Wash
In the basement sink,
ugly and utilitarian, I scrub
the dark dirt and oil
from under my fingernails,
the end of work. If only
I knew how to rebuild
the engine of No Worry.

III. Books
They are stacked everywhere like jutting, logged trees.
Page upon page, litmus
test of learnedness—
phloem and xylem,
verb and noun. Modifier
dangling. Oh Mike, how many
will you chop through
in your eager lifetime,
slaking your thirst to know?

IV. Death

Can't live without it.
Why is there a fence
around the cemetery?
'Cause people are
dying to get in.
But seriously,
I must remember
to keep a good pair
of shoes in my closet,
something for my
children to polish
then incinerate.

V. Eyesight, Nearsight

Illegible darkness vs. solemn
spotlights of the street lamps.
Signs too, are hieroglyphic.
Suddenly I've become an old man,
I am my grandfather,
drifting his giant Cadillac
through red lights, trying to
decipher the stupid street signs,
not knowing where the hell he is.

GO TO SLEEP

—for Em and Jo

Into the nightly cage of sleep they go,
but the lock is never locked. I know they know
that I know that sleep is a cold, clear pond
they do not want to fully comprehend.
Imagine this, I tell them: A soft summer
breeze, speckled sun gleaming like glitter
on the small waves they *could* float on, crisp blue
and gently rocking. But no, they would rather
thump-kick and hand-slap their pink walls, trouble-
making sing and drum, surreptitiously
ganging together a haughty doll clique
in blanket folds, in their gorgeous, dark,
almost quiet, night-light lit no-sleep room,
where it's—*Go to sleep, girls, now!*—nice and warm.

DEAR JOSHUA

Your gruff façade with twisted barbwire
    tattoos and pose
of challenge don't scare me
    but maybe you're not
trying to be scary (yeah, sure).
    I look at your eyes and see
weariness but maybe
    you're not so maybe I am
seeing myself in those
    eyes. Just 16, you're a kid.
I don't know you, can't
    imagine what your world
is like, how your dad speaks
    to you, if you even know
your dad. I stay clear of
    your staccato arms, your sharp want
an entire galaxy can't
    contain, and I wish I could
see your future the same
    way I used to wish I could
see mine, back when I
    was your age.
The wishes I coddled
    back then were laced
in anti-hope: would I ever
    see a pretty blue sky
and not dread its darkening?
    Maybe you don't have these
questions circling and
    buzzing, angry hive
of wasps. Maybe you know
    what it's like to feel

safe all the time.

    To never reach for the door
to your house and
    find it locked, to never break
a window to get back in.

    Maybe you are
a stout cyclone
    of ambition though I don't
see great wild hope in
    your eyes, can't tell
what emotions you own and
    which own you.
Maybe you have big sweet
    dreams to carry you.
Maybe they are nightmares.
    I don't know.
So why do you perplex me so?
    Why can't I just forget you?

BULLIES

What to believe? She says
nyah nyah nyah nyah nyah nyah
and the other says
blah blah blah blah, and how
articulate they are, how supple
the give-and-take of layered messages.
They miss nothing, no nuance, not
like Mom and Dad, who can deal
only in major catastrophes, like who
forgot to give the dog her beta
blocker pill this morning,
who neglected to write the check
for the field trip to the organic
strawberry farm. And yet our girl
is getting bullied unmercifully
by *that* girl, the little freaking bitch,
not even four feet tall. But *that* one
says *ours* is the one doing the brow-
beating, the hissing at. Oh, no, not our
totally loved first daughter, the one
who likes to climb any challenge
because, like Mallory said, It is there.
O! The tears and recriminations
are myriad, infinite, the sadness
galaxy-vast, and yet there is no
simple answer, no this-plus-this-
equals-that solution. *Clang! Clang! Clang!*
goes the school bell and the doors
crank shut and what happens in there
who knows, it's a secret no one
wants to talk about, not even the damn kids,

and all official communiques
(on cheap pastel paper) are poorly
written, obfuscation and vagueness
writ large and small and with
multiple exclamations!!!!!
And still and yet and therefore alas,
every day we take her there and herd her
in with the rest of the cattle
to a bloodless and pale slaughter.
Such is the 21st century family, sub-
[*Latin: under, beneath, concerning*] urban.

DIM LANDS OF PEACE

Never use such a phrase as "dim lands of peace."
It dulls the image.
—Ezra Pound

Carrying gingerly
the colostomy bag
of my fears, I went down
to the river of courage,
drank like a man
of robust thirst, a tall,
whirling dust-dervish
of infinite angst.

And then I sojourned to see
you—Love, lovely, my
love, your beauty
as strong as my love
of rusted and dented
ephemera—holed up
in your castle of
antipathy and
moss.

Rigidly I stood
outside in the cold
wind of your
ignoring me, gazing
up at your spindly and
tall towers of profound
indifference, and,
behind me, running on

forever under the
glistening sunset,
my dim lands
of peace.

—for J. D. Frey

SEAM

Desires bloom and yearn
like they always do. You are never
satisfied, just like your father,

a shark in the harbor
slashing his way through all
those dopey seals. How unlike

your mother, who crocheted hours
on end, hunched and near-sighted,
sighing. You and he are seam

rippers, you tear and rend.
Sinews crack and separate,
like when you used to brawl,

when you fractured your fist and jaw,
those small nickels and pins
of bone. At night you ran

through the drab streets howling
like a wild dog. You kissed
the rain-glistened sidewalk,

stomped the puddles. You ground
your teeth to the searing pain,
made a fist of your shattered

hand, glory in the feeling of hurt
and the feeling that it was all
so wrong, as if someone had pulled

the main seam inside
you, had unlooped the long
junction of your body and soul,

and you knew if you went fully
with it, you'd fall apart,
into mere bolts of cloth.

ARTHROPODA, INSECTA, LEPIDOPTERA

Sleep makes the problem go away for a time, but
then: my nightly echoes, my wandering on creaky feet.

I haunt the house, a mind not grasping no mind
as the ones I love sleep and the moon slips through the blinds.

I've fallen for these lonely lulls, where I pray
to be not completely done, stuck in a rut, going nowhere,

hoarding China plastic with a bad, arrhythmic heart,
upside-down mortgage, et al, on and on, and all that.

Wandering the halls of this sturdy home, crickets outside
are singing one note love songs. Inside, the dog snores, curled

on her puffy bed. I have aspired to be a good boy, meting out careful
doses of love and angst, worry and amnesia, truth and bull.

I have raged against the current of time as if swimming in a hurricane.
I have treaded water for long stretches, pining for my delicate butterfly

of hope. Pandora-like, I have begged this creature to alight
on my lips, on my brow, to make me blink and quiet.

Not always does she come, but more and more she does.
Each time, I learn more, as hope settles in, brightens my eyes.

MONSTER POEM

The city takes hours to cool each night.
Gold shimmer, then gray, falling to black.
I sleep ragged, panting like a mangy dog.
My claw hands and club feet ache.
I draw shapes in air and dirt
but remain mute, like the Sphinx.

On this earth I won't spell
anything out. I dream
of going home, but there is
no home waiting, and I have no key.
Instead: broken glass, lost bricks
and shingles, a stained discarded tub—
these make my sad quarters,
forgotten in the woods behind
your house. I hobble close.
My femur and fibula have not
mended well, they hang akimbo.
My gait is a show of horrors and racket.

There is beauty in this world.
I have learned this from you,
going about things, in your rooms.
Brushing your hair, your mindless
glazed eyes when you read.
Yet my wants are not concerned
with love nor loveliness.
Down in my heart, in the lowest
chamber: a forever black night.
My thick neck and swollen joints
would tell you these things, but you,
you'll never see, so I cannot
demonstrate my devotion.

In the mornings, I scare the alley
dumpsters for food, then lie
in wait under the pine tree.
Your car backs from the garage fast
and whisks away, radio loud.
Once you're gone, sometimes I
venture into your yard. Brazen,
I gaze through the windows
at your abode, your cell, so well kempt:
buffed hardwoods, china
smartly stacked in open cabinets,
the walls painted energetic hues.
And I wish I could, wish I could, I wish.

III

BLIZZARD AND CROW

—after Ted Hughes

the snow   comes in

wingsnap   and whirl

ashen   dire the sky

winter is   coming it

is here   blowing

furious   white it might

bury us all   except

for Crow   he hunkers

in a tree   his black

gone   blacker

UPON READING ALL OF CHRIS OFFUTT'S BOOKS

I get it real bad:
thirst for whiskey,
a stranger's blood.

I want to carry a gun
tucked into my belt,
live in woods and

creaky slanted rooms,
skin and breath,
warm sun and cool shade,

in the holler,
in the woods.
Home never lasts

here, but there it
lingers, vivid
and hard.

USEFUL

Here's your chance to be useful, she said, but it was
no use. I slithered under the house, around foundation
struts and decrepit black pipe.

Sebastian the cat was under there, but he and I were two
magnets negative to negative, so when I hunkered
closer, those red eyes hissed and receded.

Sweat bloomed all over me, the flashlight sputtered,
the earth sandpapered my knees and elbows and she
coached and advised but I could not

get any closer. As I lay, not dying but entombed,
recumbent between the two—precious woman, precious cat,
their mutual devotion an unseen filament

I could have plucked like a guitar string, a love song
I'd always be deaf to—I was completely, totally, lost.
Stuck under a house, in the crawl space between earth

and abode, girl and cat, hoping for one
of them to call me near and nuzzle me in the way
all men need to be nuzzled, lost boys we all are.

TO SYLVIA PLATH

In my head a voice recites your lines.
Your blacks crackle and drag and interrupt
the joy of the swing band music,

alas, their brass can never last. Too full, too rich,
it carries me to tears, fleeting yet shameless.
The band is crowded into the gazebo,

the sun gold and dying, pure heat.
Off in the distance, two men push a cart, gab
in Spanish. From them a boy buys

a can of lemonade. In the distance,
a blue fountain shimmers in the center
of the brown lake. August is here in full

and I am getting used to this sort of thing.
Your summer bees have drowsed and are
lazy, their compass is shot. Everyone

I love is either buried, or far away.
Your old colossus remains
on the hill, and never will get put right.

Like you, I am morbidly cloaked. Like always.
Lemonade and sweet music
force a momentary stay, little more.

This morning, I read "Edge," I read "Balloons."
I saw you with those people and the bees,
your thumb with the bloody cut.

I don't expect a miracle, or accident.
Far away from here, someone is
leaving a pebble on your stone.

THE RETURNING PATRIARCH

Away from the cauldron city,
down along the far highway.
I know you want to know, I know
you know, so let's not talk about it.
Blasted went the shape of the casino,
dust blowing on up to heaven.
What was our song, again?
Never mind. You never did care
for those small tendernesses,
when I was all about treating
you good. On my knees, lighting
candles in the church,
making all them prayers for you.

Wax the long desert of the legs,
sing the standard, chop the celery stalk,
delve it into the Bloody Mary,
swirl the tinkling red.

I go away, you know. I went
away. To Vegas.
For a few more than a couple years.
I came back in a new Cadillac
and a smart fedora and I kissed
the cheeks of the shocked kids.
You? Well, not so much.
First year back, the crows caucused
in the varicose trees
and the pool pump gurgled
and spit and you never said boo.

Life of leisure, life of spitting
out the pits, blown away, baby.
I got many stories to tell,
you know, but I'm gonna stay mute.

I done my best. I cooked, I cleaned,
painted the house, kept my mouth
shut. I windexed the windows
with crumpled newspaper
but I left a dead fly on the sill,

so what, so shoot me.
Now the dawn coming up
in those windows is perfect, babe:
burnt orange, killer blue. It shocks
the house, and slow I creep around,

bad backbone, rickety old man,
which I am. Back home I am.

SOLO RENGA

Vacation was great,
floating in the blow-up boat,
cooking in the sun.

The sun sets. Sprinklers burst on.
They arc white and blur, then die.

We buried the bird
in an orange Nike shoebox,
which the dog dug up.

Dog howls and hides in closets
every 4th: firecrackers.

Uncle lights the wick.
Cherry bomb obliterates
my model airplane.

Uncle's a Vietnam vet.
He tries, but can't, keep a job.

All work and no play
makes Ted the dullest of boys—
round face, flat brown eyes.

On earth, I run fast,
or used to, before the years
made me walk slow, slow.

The thin green inchworm crawls up
my girl's thumb: wiggly hitch-hike.

I shot a bullet
straight through my poor brother's hand.
He was waving, *Hi*.

If you must go, please wear your
new shoes, or my heart will break.

My heart goes and goes.
Amazing. It breaks and aches
and still: thump-thump, thump.

The Easter Bunny's too nice;
huge chocolate stash to scarf down.

A little tooth can
change the world, one sharp bite at
a time. (Incisor.)

Father Naumann: straight-laced. Tall.
Grave. Jesuits are like that.

Why I remember
him, who knows. He surely won't
remember me, nah.

I'd drink from Lethe, become
tabula rasa. Write me

a memory, some
thing sweet, tender and bright, warm
and happy-making.

MEMOIR OF THE IMAGINED LOVED ONES

I. Morning Commute
Tomorrow will be a different story,
but today you eat your oatmeal
and drive on the highway
always wanting to be a mile
ahead, and you tell yourself
it's all good. You tell yourself
you don't need to get there,
you want to get there.
(You're just like your mother,
just like your father, that way.)

II. *Round and Round*

In the cinderblock basement, Grandmother separates
whites from darks as the washer shudders and hums.

Your sisters cue up The Beatles,
set the needle down, scratch and pop.

They roller skate. The darks go in.
Water roils the drum, sisters spin round and round.

Grandmother pulls armfuls from the dryer.
She folds and stacks,

backbends and sighs. The girls roll
away, sing and strut.

In the kitchen, she lights a Vantage 100.
Silver ropes snake toward the hanging lamp,

and the Beatles wanna hold her hand,
the Beatles know she's been treated bad, misery,

they want her to please please them, yeah,
like they please her.

III. Men Who Drive

Grandfather and Jimmy Hoffa are buddies, former greasy knuckled truck drivers, thick biceped, undiplomaed. They will fuck you up if you cross them. Jimmy has an entourage. Grandfather has a pearl-handled stiletto. Razor sharp, he says the blade is almost as long as his dick. You've only seen him cut an apple with it.

IV. All Too Common Story
We all lose our mothers three times.
First, cleaving from the womb.
Second, the breast, third, internment.
(In between, the years float and wallow.)
It's an old story. Let us recite it by heart:
Black coffee, some smokes, brutal
icy morning. Our mothers trudge off
to a crap job, compartmentalize on adding
machines, sing-song speak into phones
with spongy shoulder rests.

And so it goes. In our heads
years blow by in montage,
the frigging script followed word
for word, page by page,
not *make it new*
but garish rerun of gray rain.

And then: overhead shot. Bright sun, summer.
We marvel at the pert rectangle
carved into the earth,
us in sharp suits and stiff shoes—
Alas, poor Yorick, but what else
does Hamlet say? Double alas!
Fuck, we are bad memorizers, but we are
learning: how soil crumbles
in our hand, the sick-sweet
scent of lilies, the one flower
our mothers despised.
The sun rages, but the dome of heaven
is crayon blue—what's it called again?

Aquamarine. Sure, we remember *that.*
Look, there: a frighteningly large spider
spindles across the brass coffin handle
we were just holding, and then

V. What Happens Next
they crank her down into the open maw of earth.
Across the road, the field where we played baseball
(poorly), the rickety stands where she used to sit and cheer us on.
Goodnight moon, goodnight mush, goodnight air, goodnight
     nobody.

VI. Wishes

Grandfather gave you a brand new
.22 rifle for your 6th birthday.
He rolled up in a white Eldorado
you hadn't seen before,
stood in the doorway,
blocked out light, said,
When you get older we'll go hunting.
Mama's boy, you whined too much
for anyone's taste.
Played with dolls. Wept
uncontrollably in the theatre
watching *The Elephant Man* with your mother,
holding her hand.
O why didn't he give you
an iron jaw, some big *cogliones*
instead of the blonde-wood rifle,
instead of the couple hundred
slaps upside the head, instead
of the 10s and 20s fat-thumbed
from a wad of cash?

VII. History of Eyeglasses

Grandmother sits in the dark kitchen, smoking.

[Voiceover: *Every memory a patina of cigarette smoke.*]

[*Exterior. Night.*]
Cricketsong, slivermoon,
middle of July.
Your mother, a teen,
enters the living room,
hours past curfew.
The shouting begins.
You worthless whore, he says,
Fuck you, daddy, she says and waits
for it, hard slap
across the mouth.

[Voiceover: *Whenever you made an unhappy face, she'd say
through a tight mouth: wipe that puss off your face.*]

[*Close shot.*]
Her eyeglasses snap and fly away
into a dark corner.
[*Jump cut.*]
Grandmother pulls another drag
with the glowing tip like Bogart
in a poster you used to own in college
and this night is something
that takes place in
the miserable room
you always find yourself lying in.

[Voiceover: *The lesson, stuck real good
in the brain of her, now in the brain of you.*]

VIII. The Facts of Running
You step into the night and run,
but are you running to or away?
Footfalls slap and a black scruff-cat
hep-tos back to the shadows and
you start slow—metaphor of life—
then pick it up. Silly bag o'
bones and cartilage, slow-twitch
fibers, clean capillaries,
tidal-rising. You make a machine
of your body just to run a circle
through the city, always coming
back to the crooked front step where
you stretch and listen, sweat-cooled,
shaky-legged, for the coming train
of sleep, hushed and rolling, far away.
You will always be trying to love it,
all of it, never will run away from it.

BUTCHER IN THE NURSING HOME

A strong bone in the crypt of meats I am.
The butcher's got blood under his nails,
blood fleck on his cheek from shaving
his own or some flank of I don't know what.

Down the hall you go, past the big ficus
you'll find him. Tell him he still owes me
money, the bastard, tell him I'm coming
for him. Tell him his ribeye's boot leather,

I want filet, thick as a manly chin.
When you get there don't slip on the floor,
the blood's all over, pink waterfall
spilling over the threshold messing up

the hall. That's the way it always is, and
above your head there will be hooks and fly
strips and a dented scale, platter on a chain,
blind like justice. Make sure he keeps his fat

thumb off it. Speaking of, you seen my ring
finger? It was here a minute ago.
I stuck my hand in the goddamn snowblower
to get a rock out and away it flew,

bloodsplat snowlawn. Matchlight
sulfurburn. I didn't look for it.
Drove to St. Mary's, parked on the street.
Got red all over the velour of the Caddy.

Don't forget now, down the hall to your right,
past them women in their frumpy shoes.
Tell him I sent you, watch him tremble
in his boots, watch him shake 'cause a me.

TORNADO

I was sleeping on the porch loveseat
when the neighbor stepped by on her way
to the bus stop, heels tapping
a beat pleasing and spare.

Then I was sitting up and a steady rain
was falling, though the sun loomed in the east.
The TV ticker-taped storm warnings
so I climbed into a cardboard box,

the box alighted and I spun into the sky,
tornado incorporating me, whirlwind
and rough. I feared that when it gave out I would
crash down, but I flew above the power lines,

above the streets, landed soft back on the porch.
A jar of ketchup had smashed there.
Thick odor of tomatoes
and ozone twitched my nose.

My grandmother phoned
from somewhere. She was afraid.
The sky is so black, she said,
and I have nowhere to go.

My sisters were nestled in the house,
busy with something. I couldn't trouble
them. I thought of the bathtub,
the southwest cellar corner, but didn't

coach her, my frail, silver-haired grandmother.
I'm on my way, I said. *I'll be there soon.*

INCESSANTLY

My daughters huff dandelion seeds
at my face and the air is all fuzzy
miniature parachutes, and so
I must produce a loud
fake sneeze. They love to make
me do such things. They collect
more and do it again, the weak stems
collapsing on themselves, white
milk ooze, the park made a weed
bed, and when they both run away
they are not the butterflies
whose wings in turn will whip up
a typhoon off the coast of Japan
or the stomp of a polar bear
that washes away the pillared
legs of a house in Key West,
but each girl is in this world
a spirit that surely knocks me
to my knees with gale force
winds and tidal washes.

AFTERGLOW

The moment after a short spill
of snow, the sky still blue, a shelf
of cloud to the north, wanting
to glide across to our yard
but not able, not yet, anyway.
Cinderella is waltzing
on the tube in the other room,
the kids are chowing popcorn,
and you are somewhere,
trotting with the dog. Just now
there are flakes haunting again
the air, a dizzy array, but I still
see blue sky to the west. As I wait
for you, I listen to Cinderella sing,
and the light outside has suddenly
warmed, and all is all happy, bright,
and I don't know how or why
grace has come to me like this,
but I am going to take whatever
I can get and question none of it.

POEM BEGINNING WITH LINES FROM BOB DYLAN

In the room the heat pipes just cough
and the country music station plays soft,
and I cannot find anything to turn off,
so when the film projector jams
I am too late. That sad burn-and-peel
of the home movie lives I once knew—
my first two-wheeled bike ride,
my sisters and I leaping into a pool,
or, before my time, Mom and Dad's
after-wedding dash to a green car
tailed with stringed cans,
all in a faded Kodachrome field.
The celluloid has bubbled and smoked
away and broke, leaving me
to wander white blaze with whirring fan.
How strange as each dawn the sky
turns blue and I'm reminded of the dead
cold mornings when I used to pray
for the earth to let me go.
Now I pray I will have all the time
I'll need, before I'm found again
in the tiny wood-paneled rooms
of the old house on McKinley Parkway
as those old pipes cough and clank,
where country music plays soft, twangy
and sweet on an old radio somewhere,
and when my mother brings me
some tea my grandmother
will stand in the doorway and ask
if I am hungry, do I want something to eat,
while there in the living room,
where the TV is forever on,

in the light cast by a reading lamp
my grandfather makes
his way through a newspaper
without a date on it.

NOTES

The band The Smiths play a large part in the poem in which they are named; it is sprinkled with lyrics from various songs, most of which appear on *Hatful of Hollow*, which I bought as a cassette tape sometime in the fall of 1985.

The poem "Like Emily Dickinson" was inspired by the poetry of one of my undergraduate professors, James Longenbach—in subject matter and tone, line length and mood.

The phrase "most prettiest" in "Birth Order" was coined by my sister, who is a model in New York City. And yes, she is the most prettiest. Each of my four sisters is most prettiest.

In reference to "Chains": our dog does have a pacemaker, with a battery pack lodged in her neck.

The Peace Bridge—pictured on the cover of the book—is just north of Buffalo, New York, and spans the mouth of the mighty Niagara River at the eastern terminus of Lake Erie, some 14 miles upstream of Niagara Falls. What goes under that bridge eventually cascades— quickly, violently—over the Falls.

The title "A Cracked Polystyrene Man" is lifted directly from a Radiohead song.

"Expectations" is the exact text of an email sent from amazon.com when trying to purchase a My Little Pony for one of our daughters.

"Blizzard and Crow" is inspired by the book *Crow*, by Ted Hughes.

A few phrases in "To Sylvia Plath" are taken directly from "Edge," one of the last poems Plath wrote. There is some debate over what she meant by "blacks crackle and drag" but the consensus is that she's creating an image of stage curtains closing—on the final act of her life, perhaps. Others think it's a reference to robes of mourning, since the speaker's children have died. "I do not expect a miracle or an accident," is a line from an earlier poem, "Black Rook in Rainy Weather."

The last lines of section V in "Memoir of the Imagined Loved Ones" are from the classic children's book, *Goodnight Moon*, which I had never read (or had read to me) until I had my own kids.

The first line in "Butcher in the Nursing Home" is borrowed from Mary Karr's poem, "Song in the Key of K." "Butcher" is a dramatic monologue in the voice of a man much like my grandfather. In fact, elements of my grandfather appear in several poems. A Teamster and friend of Jimmy Hoffa, he did lose part of his ring finger in a snowblower. He also carried a stiletto, never used a wallet, always had a wad of cash in his pocket. He loved going to the butcher shop each week and all the butchers knew him well.

"The Tornado" is pretty much an accurate portrayal of a dream I had after spending some time reading Mark Strand's *New Selected Poems*.

ACKNOWLEDGMENTS

I am indebted to so many, not only for their advice and encourage-
ment in writing this book, but for their friendship, camaraderie,
and the magic of their writing. Much appreciation to many fellow
poets that I call friends, including John Brehm, Roger Wehling,
Ginny Hoyle, J Diego Frey, David Rothman, and to my teachers,
Jarold Ramsey, John Skoyles, and Gail Mazur. And infinite gratitude
to Kimberly McClintock and David Wroblewski for their close
reading of the manuscript, helping to bring it into focus. Most
of all, I'm deeply indebted to Chris Ransick, whose feedback was
instrumental in getting these poems out into the world and into
close relationship with one another, which is never an easy task.

As always, infinite gratitude and affection goes to my wife,
Andrea Dupree, for her encouragement, her smarts, and her gen-
eral wonderfulness, and for being the most talented writer and
brilliant person I know. And to my daughters Emerson Joy and
Joanna Grace, who inspire me with their unique ability to turn
every day a beautiful gift.

In memory of Bill Knott, Cort McMeel, and Jake Adam York.
Requiescat in pace